Animal Opposites

# Smooth
## and
## Rough

## An Animal Opposites Book

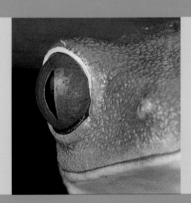

by Lisa Bullard

consulting editor: Gail Saunders-Smith, PhD
content consultant: Zoological Society of San Diego

Capstone
press

Mankato, Minnesota

Some animals have smooth fur
or slippery skin. Other animals
have rough skin or bumpy shells.

Let's learn about smooth and rough by looking at animals around the world.

# Smooth

Tree frogs have
smooth, moist skin.

American toads have rough, bumpy skin.

# Smooth

Platypuses have smooth fur everywhere except on their bills and feet.

Platypuses and echidnas are mammals that lay eggs.

Echidnas are rough
and spiny. Some people
call them spiny anteaters.

# Smooth

Sea otters have smooth fur
that keeps them warm
in cold water.

Rough shells protect
the soft bodies of crabs.

# Smooth

Butterflies fly with smooth, brightly colored wings.

# Rough

Rough spines help protect caterpillars from danger.

A caterpillar is not a caterpillar forever. Through metamorphosis it changes into a beautiful butterfly.

# Smooth

Golden lion tamarins
have smooth, silky fur.
These monkeys swing
through rain forest trees.

# Rough

Caimans have rough, bumpy skin. They swim in rain forest rivers and lakes.

# Smooth

Smooth skin helps dolphins
swim quickly through water.

# Rough

Rough spines protect
spiny puffer fish. Bigger fish
stay away from their spikes.

# Smooth

Koalas have smooth fur.
These fuzzy animals live
in Australia's trees.

Thorny devil lizards live
in Australia's deserts.
Rough, dry skin protects
them from the hot sun.

# Smooth

Smooth, thick fur keeps snow leopards warm as they hunt.

18

# Rough

Rough spines protect hedgehogs from other animals. They look too prickly to eat.

A hedgehog curls up in a ball when it's scared.

# Smooth

Jellyfish are smooth and squishy. But don't touch one. They sting.

# Rough

Sea stars usually have rough skin. They are also called star fish.

If a sea star loses an arm, it grows a new one.

# Smooth

Minks are smooth.
Fur keeps these
mammals warm.

# Rough

Porcupines are rough.
Sharp quills cover most
of these mammals' bodies.

23

# Smooth

Smooth scales help pythons
slither across the ground.

# Rough

Rough, bumpy tortoises crawl
slowly along the ground.

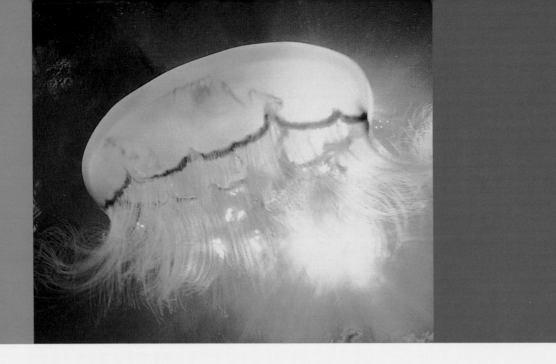

Some animals have smooth fur to stay warm and dry. Others are slick and slippery. Some animals carry around rough, bumpy shells. Others have sharp, prickly spines to keep them safe.

What kinds of smooth
and rough animals
live near you?

# Did You Know?

Frogs don't have to drink water. They take water in through their smooth skin.

If hedgehogs fall while climbing trees, they can walk away unhurt. Their spines protect them when they hit the ground.

Snow leopards and other cats have smooth fur but rough tongues. Cats clean their fur with their rough tongues. A snow leopard also uses its rough tongue to lick meat off the bones of its prey.

Many rough animals have their skeletons on the outside of their bodies. Some of these animals are crabs, grasshoppers, lobsters, and scorpions.

Prickly quills make it hard for animals to attack porcupines. But some animals, such as bobcats, flip porcupines over. They bite the porcupine's soft underside.

# Glossary

**mammal** (MAM-uhl)—a warm-blooded animal that has a backbone and feeds milk to its young; mammals also have hair; most mammals give live birth to their young.

**metamorphosis** (met-uh-MOR-fuh-siss)—the physical changes some animals go through as they develop from eggs to adults

**moist** (MOIST)—slightly wet

**prey** (PRAY)—an animal hunted by another animal

**quill** (KWIL)—a long, pointed spine of a porcupine or hedgehog

**scale** (SKALE)—one of the small, hard plates that cover the body of a snake

**spine** (SPINE)—a sharp, pointed growth on an animal

# Read More

**Kee, Lisa Morris.** *Whose Skin Is This?: A Look at Animal Skin—Scaly, Furry, and Prickly.* Whose Is It? Minneapolis: Picture Window Books, 2003.

**Miles, Elizabeth.** *Skin, Scales, and Shells.* Animal Parts. Chicago: Heinemann Library, 2003.

**Parker, Victoria.** *Rough or Smooth.* Is It? Chicago: Raintree, 2005.

# Internet Sites

FactHound offers a safe, fun way to find Internet sites related to this book. All of the sites on FactHound have been researched by our staff.

Here's how:

1. Visit *www.facthound.com*

2. Type in this special code **0736842772** for age-appropriate sites. Or enter a search word related to this book for a more general search.

3. Click on the **Fetch It** button.

FactHound will fetch the best sites for you!

# Index

A+ Books are published by Capstone Press,
151 Good Counsel Drive, P.O. Box 669, Mankato, Minnesota 56002.
www.capstonepress.com

1 2 3 4 5 6 10 09 08 07 06 05

*Library of Congress Cataloging-in-Publication Data*
Bullard, Lisa
    Smooth and rough: an animal opposites book / by Lisa Bullard.
    p. cm.—(A+ books. Animal opposites)
    Includes bibliographical references and index.
    ISBN 0-7368-4277-2 (hardcover)
    1. Body covering (Anatomy)—Juvenile literature. I. Title. II. Series.
QL941.B85 2006
573.5—dc22                                                    2004027954

Summary: Brief text introduces the concepts of smooth and rough, comparing some
    animals that are rough with some animals that are smooth.

**Credits**
Erika L. Shores, editor; Kia Adams, designer; Kelly Garvin, photo researcher;
    Scott Thoms, photo editor

**Photo Credits**
Ann & Rob Simpson, 5; Bill Johnson, 10; Brand X Pictures, 27 (bottom); Bruce Coleman
Inc./Hans Reinhard, 13, 19; Bruce Coleman Inc./Lynn M. Stone, 22; Corbis/Eric and
David Hosking, 24; Corbis/Stephen Frink, cover (right), 15; Corbis/Theo Allofs, 17;
Corel, 1 (left), 2 (top); Digital Vision, 27 (top); Digital Vision/Gerry Ellis, 2 (bottom), 26
(bottom); Digital Vision/Gerry Ellis & Michael Durham, 1 (center and right),
3 (top, bottom); Digital Vision/Stephen Frink, 26 (top); Gail Shumway, cover (left);
Getty Images Inc./John Warden, 16; Getty Images Inc./Tim Flach, 4; KAC
Productions/John & Gloria Tveten, 11; Nature Picture Library/Dave Watts, 6;
Pete Carmichael, 23; Photodisc/G. K. & Vikki Hart, 3 (middle), 27 (middle);
Seapics.com/Mark Conlin, 9; Tom & Pat Leeson, 8, 12, 14, 18, 21; Tom Stack &
Associates Inc./Brian Parker, 20; Tom Stack & Associates Inc./Dave Watts, 7;
Tom Stack & Associates Inc./Joe McDonald, 25

**Note to Parents, Teachers, and Librarians**
This Animal Opposites book uses full-color photographs and a nonfiction
format to introduce children to the concepts of smooth and rough. *Smooth and
Rough* is designed to be read aloud to a pre-reader or to be read independently
by an early reader. Photographs help listeners and early readers understand
the text and concepts discussed. The book encourages further learning by
including the following sections: Did You Know?, Glossary, Read More, Internet
Sites, and Index. Early readers may need assistance using these features.